Peyton Manning
A Football Star Who Cares

Barry Wilner

Enslow Elementary
an imprint of
Enslow Publishers, Inc.
40 Industrial Road
Box 398
Berkeley Heights, NJ 07922
USA

http://www.enslow.com

Enslow Elementary, an imprint of Enslow Publishers, Inc.

Enslow Elementary® is a registered trademark of Enslow Publishers, Inc.

Library of Congress Cataloging-in-Publication Data

Wilner, Barry.
  Peyton Manning : a football star who cares / Barry Wilner.
     p. cm. — (Sports stars who care)
  Includes bibliographical references and index.
  Summary: "A biography of football player Peyton Manning, highlighting his
charitable work"—Provided by publisher.
  ISBN 978-0-7660-3774-8
  1. Manning, Peyton—Juvenile literature. 2. Football players—United States—Biography
—Juvenile literature. 3. Philanthropists—United States—Biography—Juvenile literature.
I. Title.
  GV939.M289W54 2011
  796.332092—dc22
  [B]
                              2010014946

122010 Lake Book Manufacturing, Inc., Melrose Park, IL

Printed in the United States of America

10 9 8 7 6 5 4 3 2 1

To Our Readers:
We have done our best to make sure all Internet addresses in this book were active and appropriate
when we went to press. However, the author and the publisher have no control over and assume no
liability for the material available on those Internet sites or on other Web sites they may link to. Any
comments or suggestions can be sent by e-mail to comments@enslow.com or to the address on the
back cover.

Illustration Credits: Associated Press

Cover Illustration: Associated Press

Contents

Introduction

Many people believe Peyton Manning is the greatest quarterback ever to play pro football. He is the only four-time winner of the Most Valuable Player (MVP) award, and he did that in his first twelve NFL seasons.

Manning also has been to two Super Bowls, winning one. He has taken the Indianapolis Colts from the bottom of the league to the top, and the Colts won at least ten games every season from 2002 to 2009. He soon could hold every passing record in the sport.

Since he was picked at the very top of the NFL draft of college players in 1998, Manning has started every game. That has toughened his teammates, who say, "If Peyton can play, I can play" even when they have minor injuries.

Quarterback is the most important position on offense, and Manning's leadership makes him stand out. So does his sense of humor, and he can be seen in many TV ads and in such shows as *Saturday Night Live*.

When you watch Manning in a game, you will notice how different he is from other quarterbacks. He moves around behind his offensive line, yelling out plays, pointing at defenders, changing when the ball is to be snapped. But then, BINGO, he throws for another touchdown.

Manning comes from a family of star football players. His father, Archie, was one of the best college quarterbacks ever and then played thirteen seasons in the NFL. Peyton's older brother, Cooper, was a receiver at the University of Mississippi until an injury ended his career. Youngest brother, Eli, also went to Ole Miss, and now quarterbacks the New York Giants. Eli Manning won the 2008 Super Bowl—just one year after Peyton Manning won his first championship.

Peyton Manning had become known as a great quarterback who could not win the Big One. To join the very best who ever played, he needed a Super Bowl ring. Winning the NFL championship is the best thing any player can do in pro football. In his first eight seasons with the

Chapter 1

Super Season

Indianapolis Colts, Manning had won eighty games, lost only forty-eight, and led his team to four division titles and six playoff appearances.

But they were only 3–6 in playoff games, and people began wondering if Manning would ever win it all.

Manning hands the ball off to teammate Joseph Addai for a running play against the Baltimore Ravens in their playoff game in January 2007.

"To be considered a true success in football, you have to win a championship, maybe a few of them," Manning said. "That's how you are measured."

In 2005, the Colts had the NFL's best record, 14–2, but fell to Pittsburgh in their only playoff game. Making it worse for Manning, the Steelers went on to win the Super Bowl.

So when the 2006 season began, Manning and the Colts wanted to earn the Vince Lombardi Trophy that goes to the NFL champion.

Peyton led the Colts past his younger brother, New York Giants' quarterback Eli Manning, in the season opener. They won their next eight games, too. They even beat the New England Patriots, who had won three Super Bowls in four years while Indy was searching for its first.

When the Colts lost four of their last seven contests, the doubters again were heard loud and clear. They said the Colts were a good team, but one that always fell short. They said the same thing about Manning.

Peyton Manning celebrates after leading the Colts on the game-winning drive against the Patriots in the AFC Championship game on January 21, 2007.

Then he won a playoff game against Kansas City. And another against Baltimore. In the AFC championship game, with the winner going to the Super Bowl, guess who stood in the Colts' way? The Patriots. This time Manning would. This time, Manning would not let his team fail.

Head Coach Tony Dungy looks on as Manning raises the Lombardi Trophy after the Colts win the Super Bowl.

New England led 21–3 late in the first half before the Colts got a field goal. Manning then was unstoppable in the second half, three times leading Indy back into tie scores before guiding it to the winning touchdown. The Colts scored 32 points in the second half to win 38–34—and head to their first Super Bowl.

"That second half was as great as anyone can play," teammate Reggie Wayne said of Manning.

There was more to come. Many players in their first Super Bowl might be nervous, unable to focus on the game. With all the attention on Manning, could he answer the critics?

You bet.

Manning was the MVP of the Super Bowl XLI win over Chicago, throwing for 247 yards and a touchdown in the rain. When he was handed the Lombardi Trophy, it looked like Peyton Manning would never let it go.

When Peyton Manning was growing up in New Orleans, his was not yet the First Family of Quarterbacks. Sure, his father, Archie, was an All-American at the University of Mississippi and then an NFL star with the Saints.

Chapter 2

The Young Quarterback

New Orleans Saints quarterback Archie Manning looks to make a pass during a game against the Los Angeles Rams in November 1973.

Someday, Peyton believed, he might be able to do a few of the things his father did.

From the beginning, Peyton had a strong drive to be a winner. Archie likes to tell the story about driving his son home from a T-ball game Peyton's team lost. His coach always told his young players that the games ended in a tie.

"Dad," Peyton said to Archie, "the coach must think we're pretty stupid."

Peyton was not going to be the first young Manning to follow Archie's path, though. His brother Cooper was two years older and would beat Peyton at most everything when they were young. All of the Manning boys—Eli is five years younger than Peyton—were very good students and close friends as well as brothers, but, well, boys will be boys, and there was a rivalry between Cooper and Peyton.

"Peyton liked to tell on Cooper, like, 'Mommy, Cooper did so and so,'" his mom, Olivia, said.

What Cooper did was play quarterback in elementary school; Peyton was the team manager

Peyton and his father talk to reporters before a big game.

until he was old enough to play. By high school, Cooper had become a wide receiver at Isidore Newman School. Why the switch?

Easy—Cooper knew that Peyton would be a better quarterback.

And he was—very quickly.

As a freshman at Newman, Peyton got some advice from a former pro QB: his dad.

"People are going to compare you to me in high school," Archie Manning said. "And when you go to college, they're going to compare you to whoever came before you, and to me."

Quite a challenge, one that Peyton met head-on.

Tenth-grader Peyton and his brother Cooper led Newman to the state final four, even though Newman is a private school and was playing against much larger public schools. Peyton completed 140 passes, with Cooper catching 80 of them.

"That season brought us together as brothers," Cooper said.

Archie, Peyton, Cooper,
and Eli Manning together
at a black-tie affair in
May 2007.

Then they were separated as Cooper headed to Ole Miss, where Archie Manning had played college football.

In his final two years at Newman, Peyton was unstoppable. He was selected the 1993–94 Gatorade National Football Player of the Year, beating out thousands of other high schoolers. He led Newman to a 34–5 record during his three seasons as the starting quarterback and finished with 7,207 yards passing and 92 touchdowns.

Best of all, because of Archie's tie-in with the Saints, Peyton was able to watch the team practice while he was in high school. He even got to throw some passes to Saints receivers.

That's when Saints head coach Jim Mora told Archie he believed Peyton would become a star quarterback in the pros.

But first, college.

Peyton Manning had a very difficult choice to make as he was finishing high school. His father, Archie, was one of the all-time greats at the University of Mississippi; the most popular player Ole Miss ever had. Archie was a quarterback, and if Peyton

chapter 3

A Volunteer

Tennessee quarterback Peyton Manning looks for an open receiver during a game against Kentucky on November 18, 1995.

went to Mississippi, he knew he would always be compared to his dad.

Still, Peyton's older brother, Cooper, went to Ole Miss as a wide receiver. Cooper had to quit football, though, because of a neck injury.

After thinking about his decision for many months, Peyton chose the University of Tennessee, a rival of Ole Miss in the Southeastern Conference.

"I didn't want to go anywhere where I would be a star without doing anything," he said. "That's what would have happened at Ole Miss."

At Tennessee, Manning was not a star right away. After enrolling early to learn the Volunteers' offense, he began the 1994 season as a backup. In fact, Tennessee had three other quarterbacks, and all of them got a chance to play that year.

But by the fifth game, with the Vols' record at 1–3, Manning was first-string QB. Tennessee won seven of its last eight games and won the Gator Bowl.

Manning was voted the conference's top freshman. He would start every college game

Peyton Manning is hugged by one of the Tennessee cheerleaders moments after leading the school to victory over Ohio State in the Citrus Bowl on New Year's Day, 1996.

after that, and Tennessee went from a running team to a passing team.

And why not? Coach Philip Fulmer knew just what he had in Peyton Manning.

"Can somebody be this much a gentleman? Can somebody be this intense about football? Can somebody be this smart?" Fulmer said. "He's certainly not perfect, but from a football coach's standpoint to coach a player, he's darn near perfect."

Maybe not perfect, but Manning led the Vols to 39 wins in 45 starts, an SEC championship and two bowl victories. Manning set thirty-three school records, eight conference marks and two overall college records, won the Sullivan Award as top amateur athlete in America, and the Maxwell Award as best college football player in 1997. He was runner-up to Charles Woodson of Michigan for the Heisman Trophy.

Winning the Sullivan meant the most to Manning.

Peyton drops back to throw during a game against Texas Tech on August 30, 1997.

"It's really very humbling when a person is selected to receive an award for something he loves to do," Manning said when presented with the trophy from the U.S. Amateur Athletic Union. "It's even more rewarding for me to receive the Sullivan Award . . . because its voters traditionally look beyond statistics and highlights. Instead they look at the person and what he or she represents."

Manning was only the fourth football player and the first Volunteer to win it.

"Tennessee has been good to me," Manning said after his final game, an Orange Bowl loss to Nebraska. "I can't pay them back enough . . . I'll always be a Tennessee Volunteer the rest of my life."

When Peyton Manning did not win the Heisman Trophy, it meant little to the NFL. Either the Indianapolis Colts or San Diego Chargers, the first two teams who would pick in the 1998 draft, would choose him.

Manning wanted to be the number one overall

Chapter 4

Top of The Draft

Washington State quarterback Ryan Leaf throws during practice in December 1997. Many wondered which quarterback would go first in the 1998 NFL draft: Leaf or Manning?

pick because it meant he was considered the best player in college football by those in the pro game.

"There have been some great quarterbacks taken No. 1," Manning said before the draft in New York. "Guys like John Elway and Troy Aikman and Terry Bradshaw, who's from Louisiana. I'd like to have the kind of success they have had."

Manning was such a good player in college that most NFL teams wanted him. But neither the Colts nor the Chargers were interested in a trade, knowing that Manning could be their quarterback and leader for many years—and maybe for many championships.

His main competition to be selected first overall was another quarterback, Ryan Leaf of Washington State. Manning had been a starter at Tennessee for three and a half years, though, and Leaf played far less often for the Cougars. In fact, Leaf had only one special season, when he led his team to the Rose Bowl on New Year's Day 1998. But he then skipped his senior year in college to turn pro.

Leaf had a very strong arm, was a better runner than Manning and, some believed, would be a starter sooner in the NFL. Colts president Bill Polian did not think so.

"One of the first things I noticed about Peyton was how smart he is, yet how many good

Manning holds up his new team jersey after being drafted No. 1 by the Indianapolis Colts on April 18, 1998. Standing with him are the Colts owner Jim Irsay (left), and NFL Commissioner Paul Tagliabue (right).

questions he would ask about the team and the offense," Polian said. "And another thing was that Peyton never will be outworked by anyone. His work ethic is as good as, and probably better than, any athlete or person I've met."

Still, the Colts never announced ahead of time whom they would choose. They waited for NFL commissioner Paul Tagliabue to take the stage at Madison Square Garden and say: "With the first pick in the 1998 NFL draft, the Indianapolis Colts select Peyton Manning, quarterback, University of Tennessee."

Manning did not throw his arms in the air as if celebrating a touchdown pass. He did not high-five his family. He smiled and headed onto the stage. With cameras flashing and the crowd cheering, Manning held up a No. 18 Colts jersey with his name on the back, put on a Colts baseball cap, and simply enjoyed being number one.

Of all the great players in NFL history, only one has been voted the NFL's Most Valuable Player four times: Peyton Manning.

At a time when pro football rosters have been filled with superstar quarterbacks (Brett Favre and Tom Brady),

chapter 5

Mr. MVP

Peyton Manning calls the signals during a game in September 2010.

runners (Curtis Martin and LaDainian Tomlinson), and defensive standouts (Ray Lewis and Brian Urlacher), Manning has stood above them all.

Although Manning shared the QB spot on the NFL's Team of the Decade for 2000–09 with Brady, Brady grabbed only one MVP honor. Twice, in 2003 and 2004, then in 2008 and 2009, Manning won consecutive MVPs.

Maybe the award should be renamed Most Valuable Peyton. With his fourth trophy, he joined Wayne Gretzky (nine), Barry Bonds (seven), and Kareem Abdul-Jabbar (six) as leaders for MVP awards in their sports.

Manning does not like to talk much about his success, so he lets others do so.

"He's been such a highly accomplished performer year in and year out. Just when you think you've seen his best, he improves upon it," said Jim Caldwell, who coached the Colts to the 2009 AFC title. "I think a lot of it has to do with his drive. He just has an innate sort of will to

Manning launches another big pass!

excel. He never gets bored with it. That, I think, is highly unusual."

The numbers Manning put up in his first dozen NFL seasons seem to jump off the page. He started every game in his career for those twelve years: 192 in the regular season, winning 131, and 18 in the playoffs, winning nine and one Super Bowl. He was on track to become the career leader in every important passing category and had already broken team records held by Hall of Famer Johnny Unitas, considered by some as the greatest NFL passer ever.

"Wow! That's impressive," said tight end Dallas Clark, who caught 100 passes from Manning in 2009. "But with him, you really don't get shocked too much."

Manning also is the only current NFL quarterback who calls all the plays. Watch him moving around before the snap, flapping his arms, pointing at the defense, and it seems confusing. Not to Manning, who is in total control, and

Manning scrambles from the pocket and takes off with the ball during a game against the Houston Texans.

usually picks the right play to gain yards or score a touchdown.

"It's important to me that the team has faith and confidence in me to do the right thing," Manning said. "I think it would mean a lot to every quarterback."

Few quarterbacks earn that kind of trust from their coaches, not even veterans such as Drew Brees, who led the New Orleans Saints past the Colts in the 2010 Super Bowl. Not even Peyton's younger brother, Giants' quarterback Eli Manning.

"He keeps getting better every year," said brother Eli, himself a Super Bowl winner. "I don't get jealous. He sets the standard for what I want to become, where I want to raise my level of play to."

Just about every athlete in every sport can say that about Peyton Manning.

Peyton Manning wants to pay back. He feels a duty to do so. So he started the PeyBack Foundation in 1999, his second season in the NFL. It has since grown into an organization that has donated about $4 million to youth groups in Indiana, Tennessee, and Louisiana.

Chapter 6

Making a Difference

He began Peyton's Pals in 2003. That program selects twenty teenagers each year who take part in school, cultural, and community activities. The youngsters have a bowling day, play flag football, visit other cities, and hand out items such as backpacks to children in need.

Manning also sponsors the PeyBack Classic, which allows Indianapolis public high schools to

Manning plays "Colts Trivia" with some kids during summer training camp in 2005. Manning has always recognized the importance of giving back.

play at the Colts' stadium. Money from ticket sales goes to the schools and to the foundation.

In fact, when the new Lucas Oil Stadium opened in 2009, the first football game played there was part of the PeyBack Classic.

He also makes sure that children who cannot afford tickets to Colts games get a chance to see them for free. The foundation buys fifty tickets for each home game and gives them to local groups. The kids also receive a PeyBack Foundation T-shirt.

At Thanksgiving, the foundation gives bags of groceries to hundreds of families. It also hosts holiday parties, with one at the Peyton Manning Children's Hospital at St. Vincent in Indianapolis. Peyton and family members are regulars at such functions.

Through PeyBack, Manning donates to more than a hundred youth organizations, including Boys and Girls Clubs and after-school programs.

Peyton and younger brother, Eli, might be best remembered for helping the folks in their hometown of New Orleans after Hurricane Katrina destroyed much of the city. After Katrina hit the Gulf Coast, they flew to Louisiana and delivered 30,000 pounds of relief supplies.

At the end of that year, Peyton was honored as the Walter Payton Man of the Year by the NFL.

"I challenge each and every player in the National Football League to consider the impact they have just because they play the game of football, then go do something about it," Manning said. "There's more to the game."

And there's more to Manning's charity work Manning presents the PeyBack Award each year to a current or retired player who has given back to the game and to society. Such Pro Football Hall of Famers as Gale Sayers, Roger Staubach, Dan Marino and Jim Kelly have won it.

The annual PeyBack Bowl raises nearly $400,000 that goes to disadvantaged youngsters. In the celebrity bowling tournament, NFL players and other stars team with sponsors.

Many Louisiana homes and cars were left underwater in the wake of Hurricane Katrina in 2005. Peyton Manning aided those who were victimized by the terrible storm.

"Children need opportunities through which they can learn and grow," Manning wrote in the program for the PeyBack Bowl, "and the PeyBack Foundation strives to make these experiences a reality for the kids who need them most."

Career Statistics

Year	Team	Games	Att	Comp	Pct	Yds	Td	Int
1998	Indianapolis	16	575	326	56.7	3,739	26	28
1999	Indianapolis	16	533	331	62.1	4,135	26	15
2000	Indianapolis	16	571	357	62.5	4,413	33	15
2001	Indianapolis	16	547	343	62.7	4,131	26	23
2002	Indianapolis	16	591	392	66.3	4,200	27	19
2003	Indianapolis	16	566	379	67.0	4,267	29	10
2004	Indianapolis	16	497	336	67.6	4,557	49	10
2005	Indianapolis	16	453	305	67.3	3,747	28	10
2006	Indianapolis	16	557	362	65.0	4,397	31	9
2007	Indianapolis	16	515	337	65.4	4,040	31	14
2008	Indianapolis	16	555	371	66.8	4,002	27	12
2009	Indianapolis	16	571	393	68.8	4,500	33	16
	TOTALS	192	6,531	4,232	64.8	50,128	366	181

Att = Attempts   Pct = Completion Percentage   Td = Touchdowns
Comp = Completions   Yds = Yards   Int = Interceptions

Where to Write

PEYTON MANNING
C/O PEYBACK FOUNDATION
6235 North Guilford
Suite 201
Indianapolis, IN 46220.

Words to Know

American Football Conference (AFC)—The NFL conference in which the Indianapolis Colts play.

all-pro—One of the best players in the league.

center—The player who hikes the ball to the quarterback and also is the leader of the offensive line.

defense—The act of stopping the other team from scoring.

defensive coordinator—The assistant coach in charge of the defense.

end zone—Where teams try to advance the ball to score points.

extra point—A play after a touchdown, worth one point if the ball is kicked through the goalposts, two points if it is run or passed into the end zone.

field goal—A kick, worth three points, that goes through the goalposts.

Heisman Trophy—An award given to the most outstanding college player.

home-field advantage—When a team gets to play games in its own stadium.

linebacker—A position on defense behind the line, from which players make tackles or cover receivers.

Most Valuable Player (MVP)—Award given to the best player in the league.

National Football League (NFL)—A thirty-two team league for pro football.

offensive coordinator—The assistant coach in charge of the offense.

playoffs—A series of games played after the regular season to determine a league champion.

quarterback—The player who takes the snap from the center and either hands off, runs himself, or throws the ball to other players.

rookie—A first-year player.

running back—The player who takes handoffs from the quarterback and runs with the ball.

sack—When a quarterback is knocked to the ground before he can pass the ball.

statistics (stats)—A player's key numbers, such as touchdowns, yards gained, passes completed.

Super Bowl—The championship game of the NFL.

tight end—The player who stands at the end of the offensive line and either blocks or goes downfield to catch passes.

touchdown—When a player gets into the end zone with the ball, worth six points.

veteran—A player with years of experience.

wide receiver—The player who stands to the outside when the ball is snapped and usually catches passes.

winning record—When a team has more wins than losses in a season.

Books

Crompton, Samuel Willard. *Peyton Manning*. New York: Chelsea House, 2008.

Doeden, Matt. *Peyton Manning*. Minneapolis: Twenty-First Century Books, 2008.

Sandler, Michael. *Peyton Manning and the Indianapolis Colts: Super Bowl XLI*. New York: Bearport Pub. Company, Inc., 2008.

Savage, Jeff. *Peyton Manning*. Minneapolis: First Avenue Editions, 2007.

Internet Addresses

PeytonManning.com
http://www.peytonmanning.com

Official Web Site of the Indianapolis Colts
http://www.colts.com

NFL Official Site
http://www.nfl.com/players/peytonmanning/ profile?id=MAN515097

Index